The Legend of Rosa's Window

as retold by Mark Tezel

assaca press
san antonio

The Legend of Rosa's Window
by Mark Tezel

Published by:
ASSACA PRESS
6719 Shadow Run
San Antonio, Texas 78250-1742

All rights reserved. No part of this book may be reproduced or transmitted in any form or by any means, electronic or mechanical, including photocopying, recording, or by an information storage and retrieval system without written permission from the author, except for the inclusion of brief quotations in review.

Copyright © 1999 by Mark Tezel

ISBN 0-9667687-1-X

To Mrs. Stallworth's Third Grade Class
1998-1999
Fernandez Elementary School

Many years ago, when Texas was a part of Spain, there was a bustling community near the San Antonio River called Mission San José. At first Mission San José was made up of simple buildings. As the community grew, however, the buildings became larger and made of stone. Eventually, the decision was made that the community needed a new church.

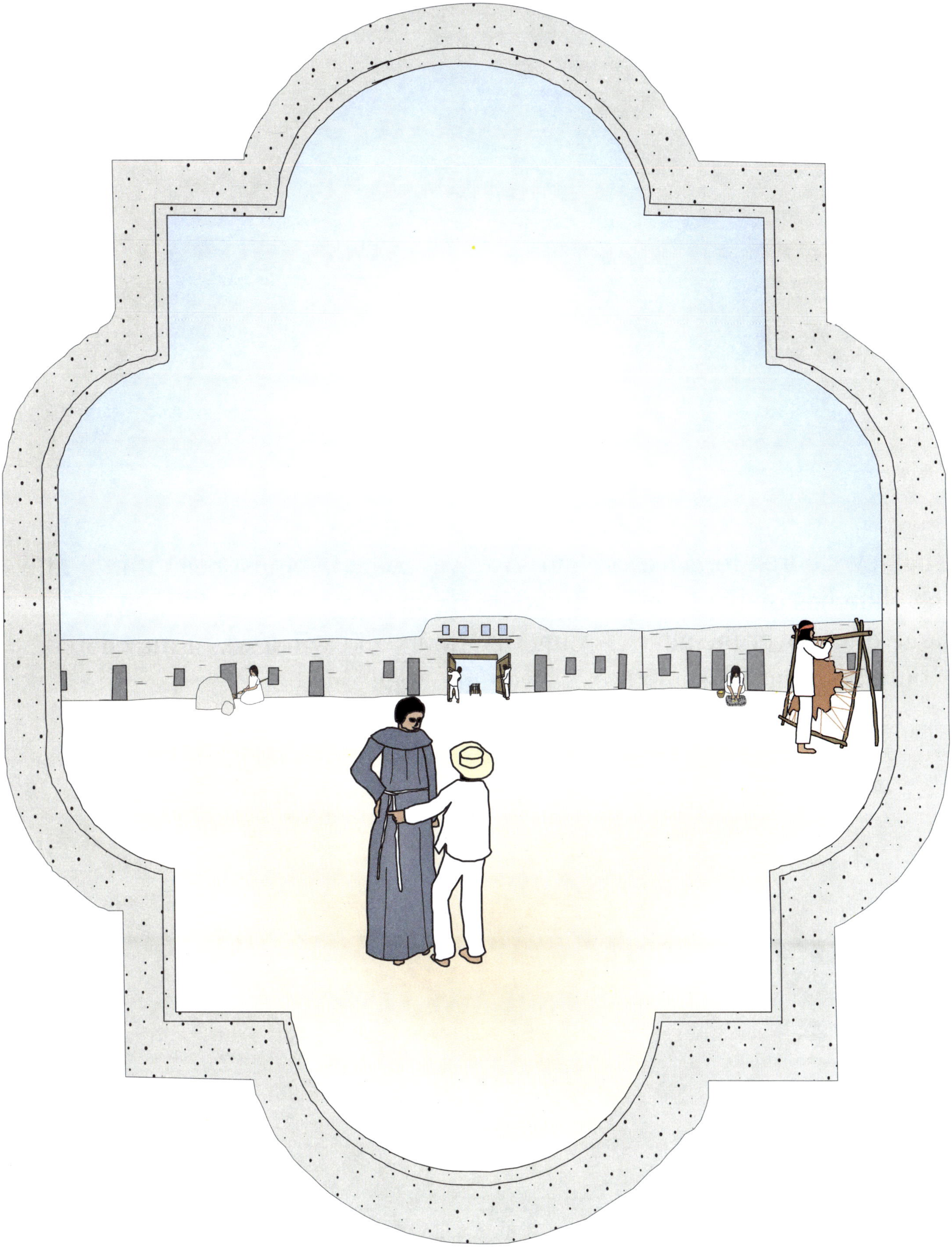

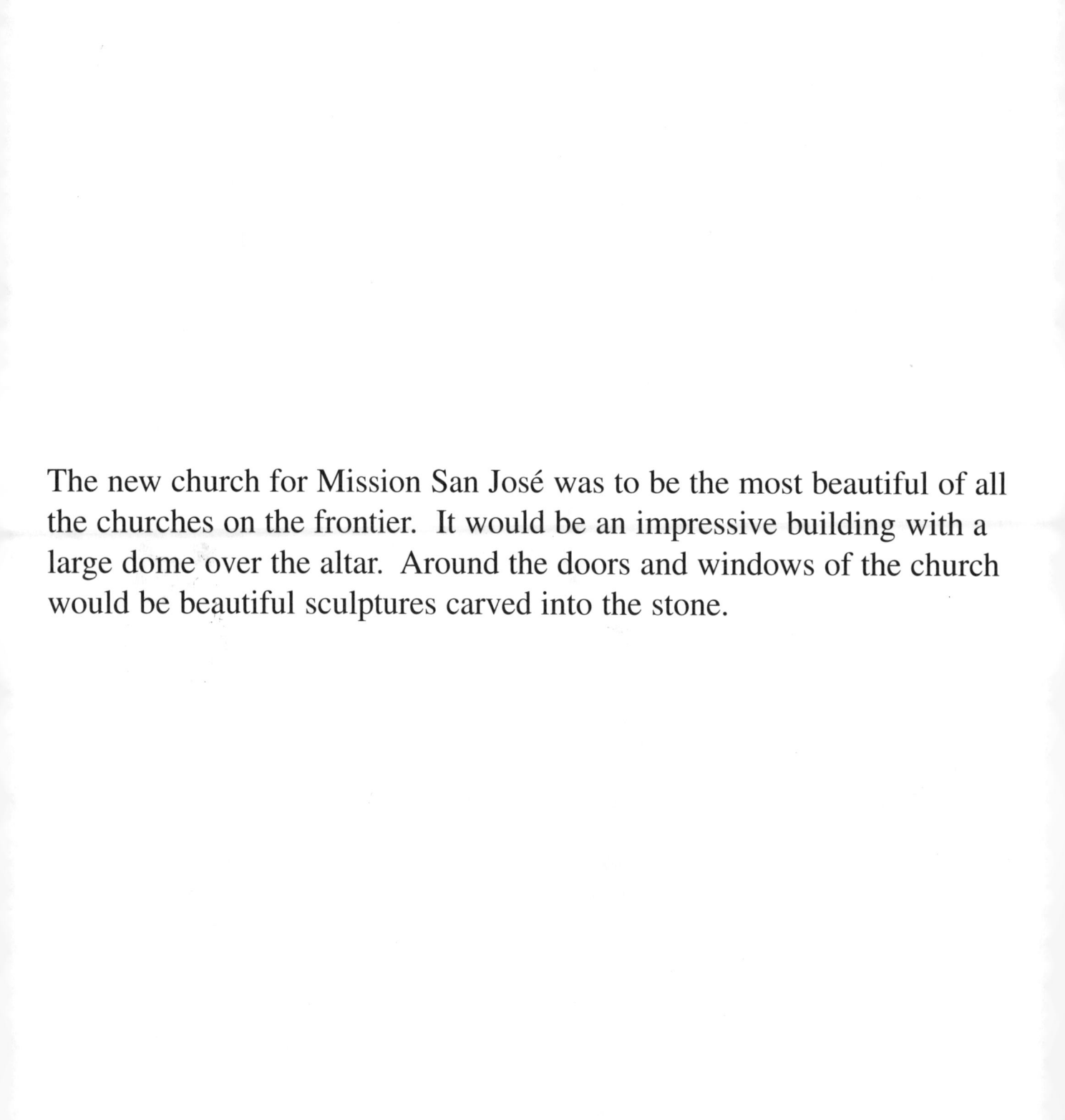

The new church for Mission San José was to be the most beautiful of all the churches on the frontier. It would be an impressive building with a large dome over the altar. Around the doors and windows of the church would be beautiful sculptures carved into the stone.

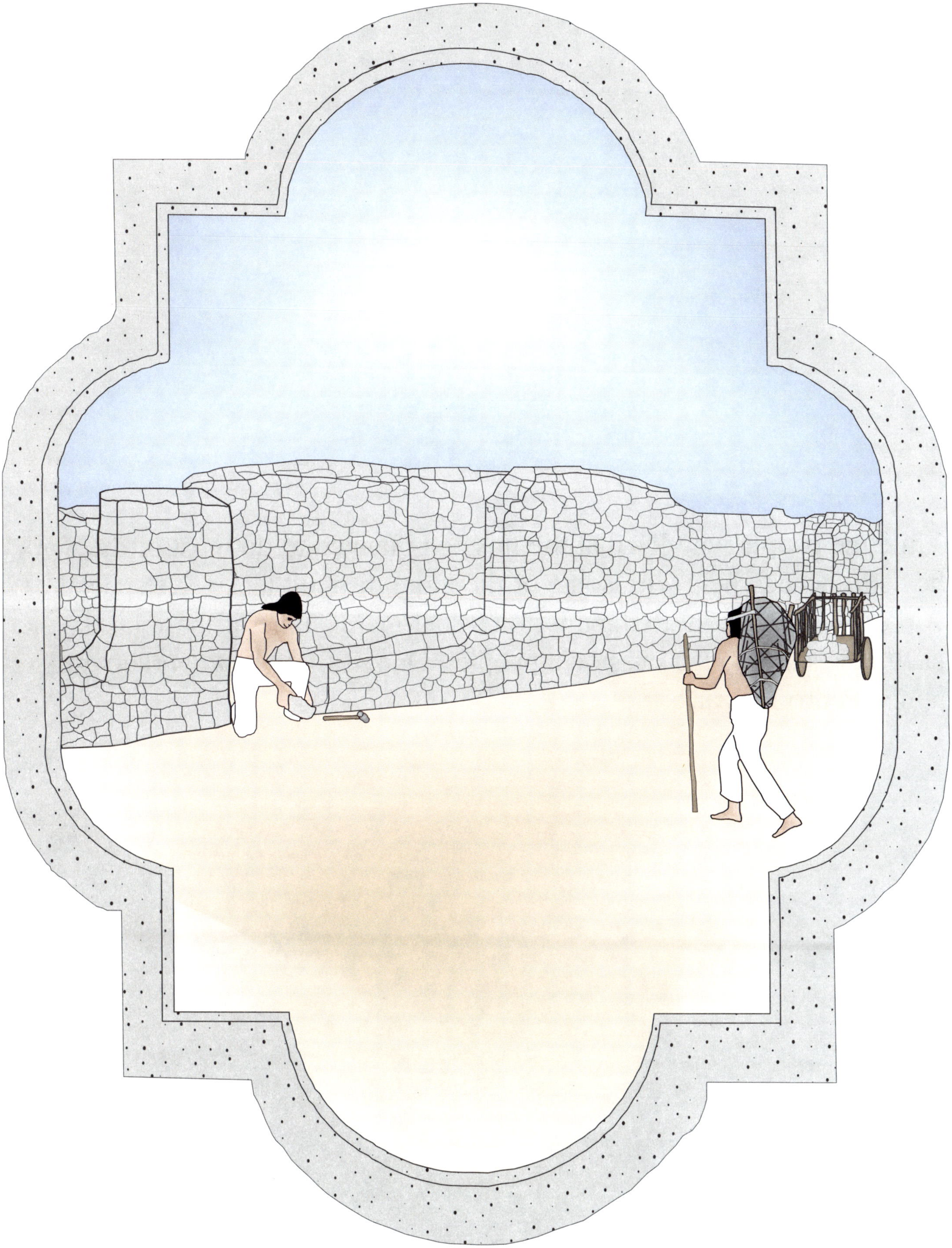

While the people who lived at the mission planned to do most of the work, they still needed help with some of the more difficult tasks. So special workers were brought to the mission to help with some of these tasks, and teach new skills to the mission's people. One of these new workers was named Pedro Huizar.

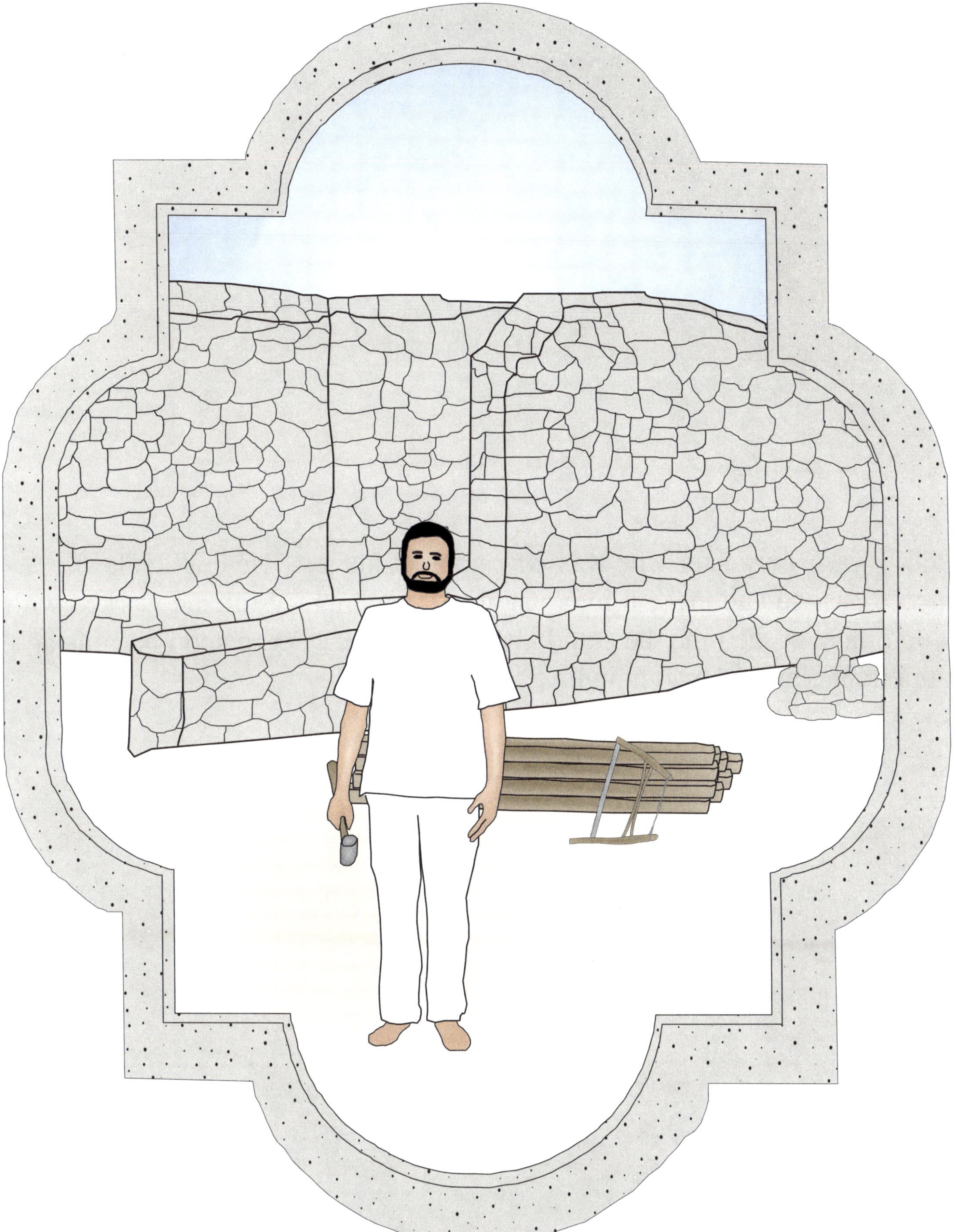

Pedro was a carpenter who was very good at his job. He could take a piece of wood and make it into just about anything. While he worked with wood most of the time, he could also carve stone. Pedro soon became an important part of the community.

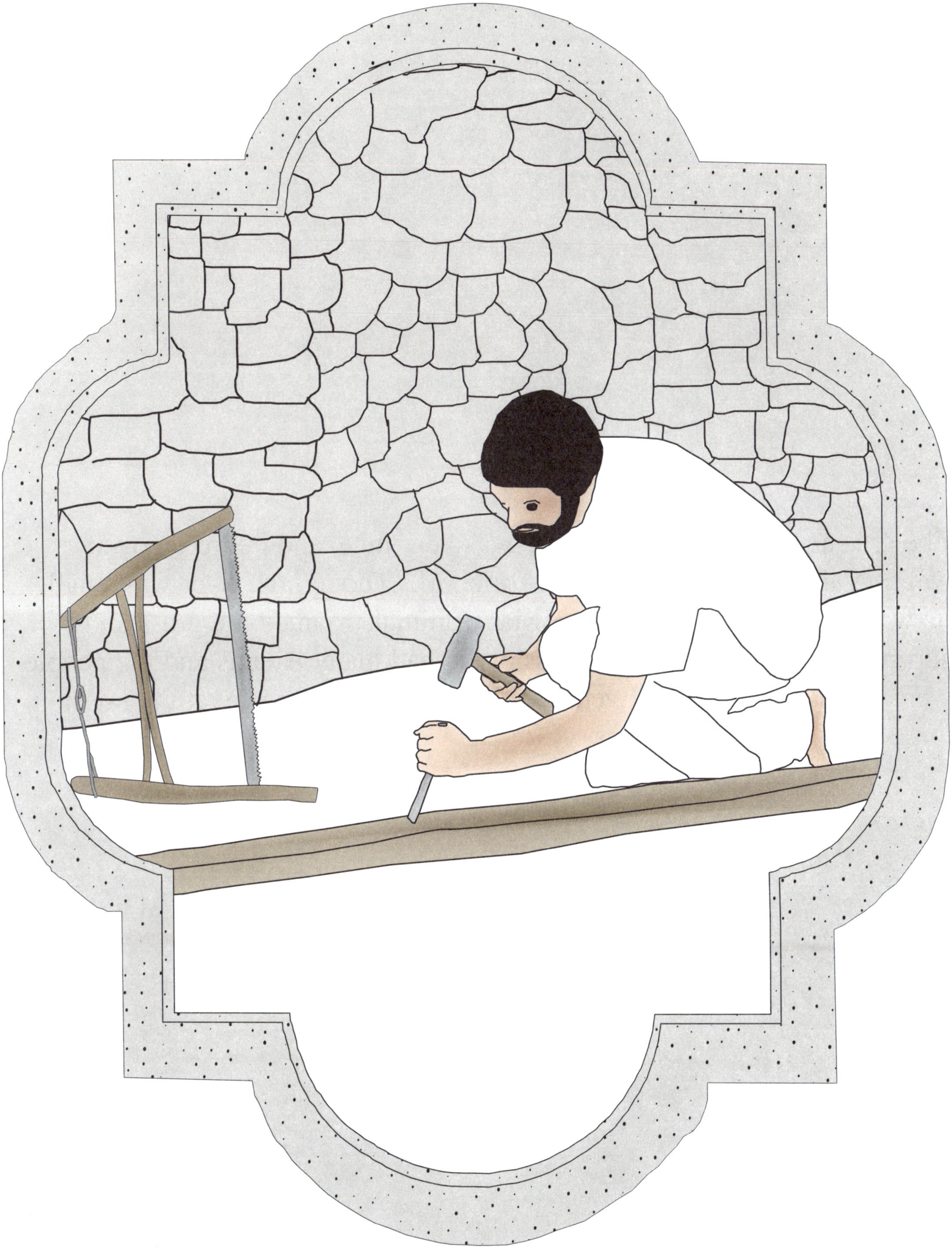

The area around Mission San José was very nice, and Pedro enjoyed walking along the river during his time off. Though the river was small, its waters were very refreshing. Many animals roamed the grasslands surrounding the river. At the mission he had many friends and the people were pleasant and kind. Eventually, Pedro decided to stay at the mission.

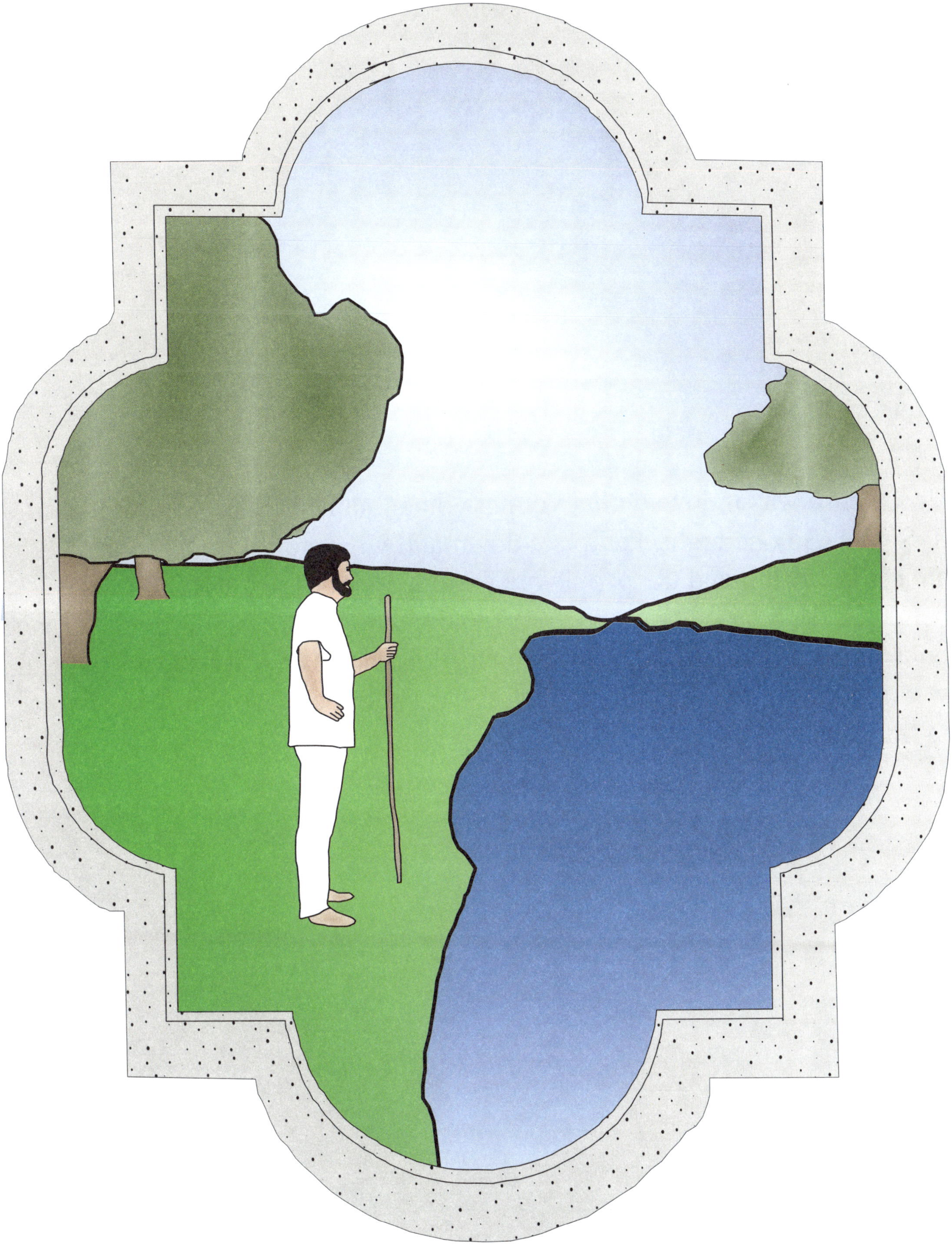

Now Pedro was in love with a young woman named Rosa, who was living in Spain. So one night, Pedro sat down and wrote to his dear Rosa: "The area is beautiful, and the people are extremely kind. I can think of no better place to raise a family. I am sending enough money to book passage on a ship. Please come here as soon as you can. We will have a beautiful wedding in the mission church, and then spend the rest of our lives living in this peaceful river valley."

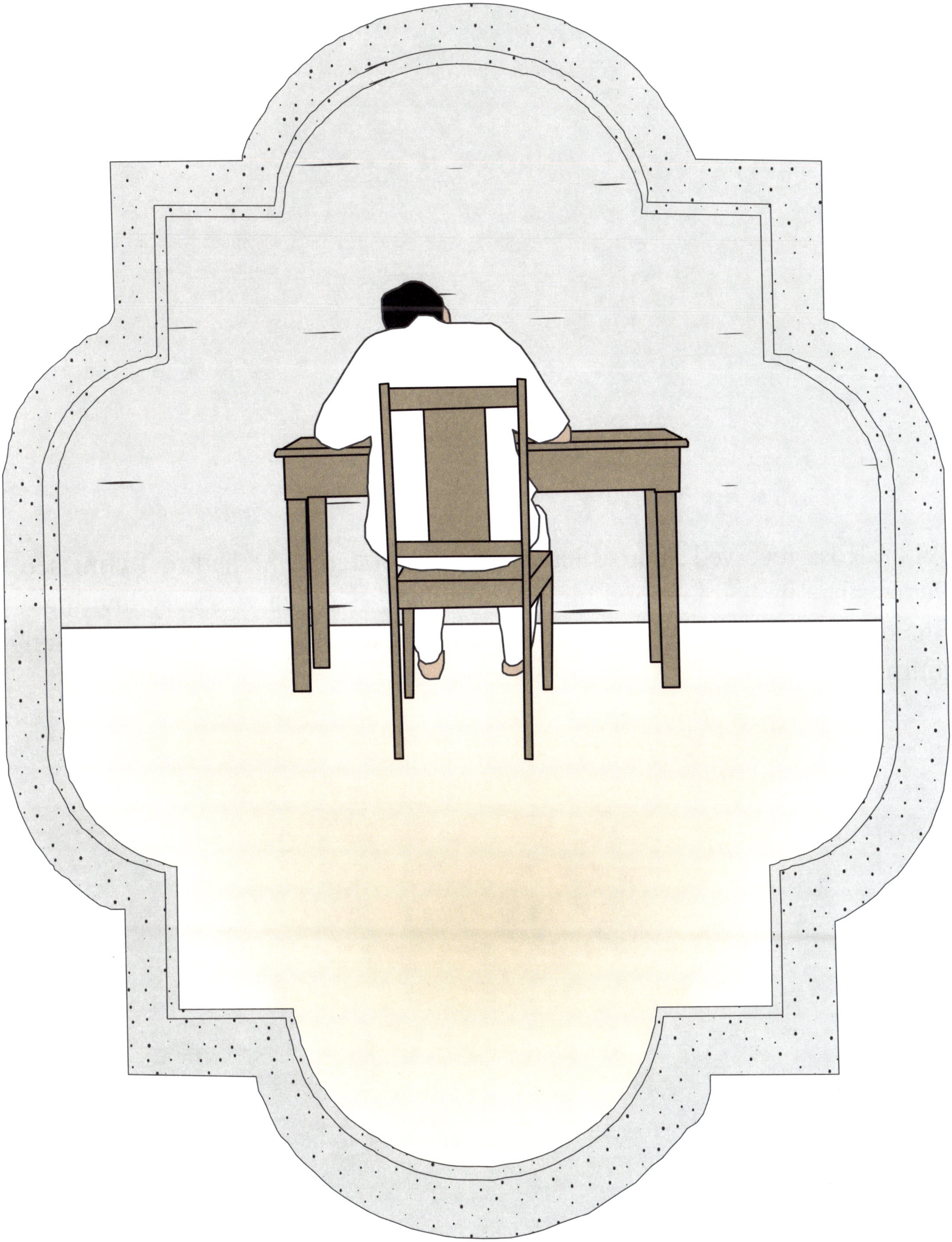

When Rosa received Pedro's letter, she was elated. She had really missed Pedro since he had left, and his description of the area was very inviting. She quickly found a ship that would take her to Texas, and started her long journey.

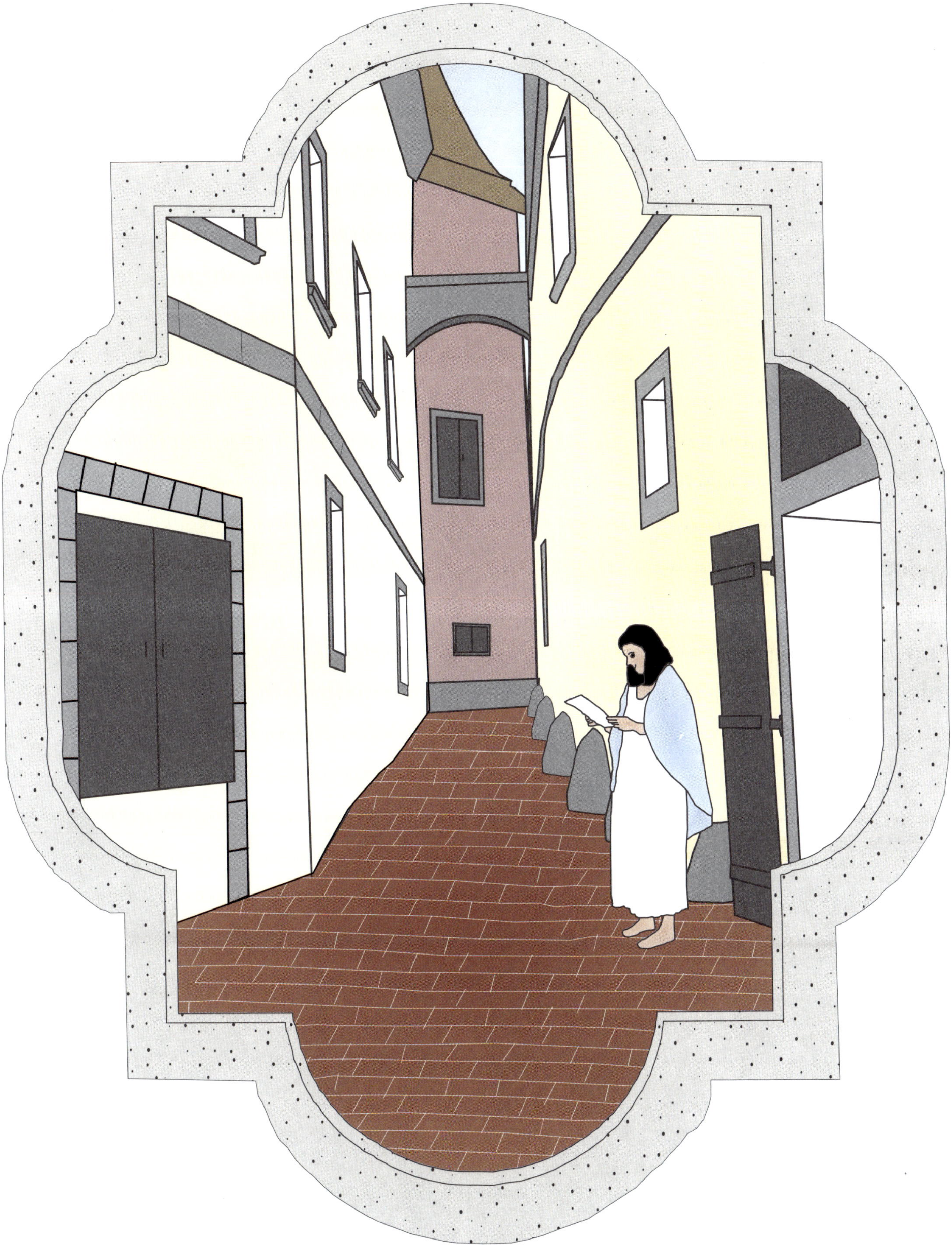

Meanwhile, back at Mission San José, Pedro was getting ready for Rosa's arrival and their wedding. He chose a beautiful spot along the river where they could build a cabin, and began to work on their new home. He could hardly wait for that wonderful day when Rosa would join him at the mission.

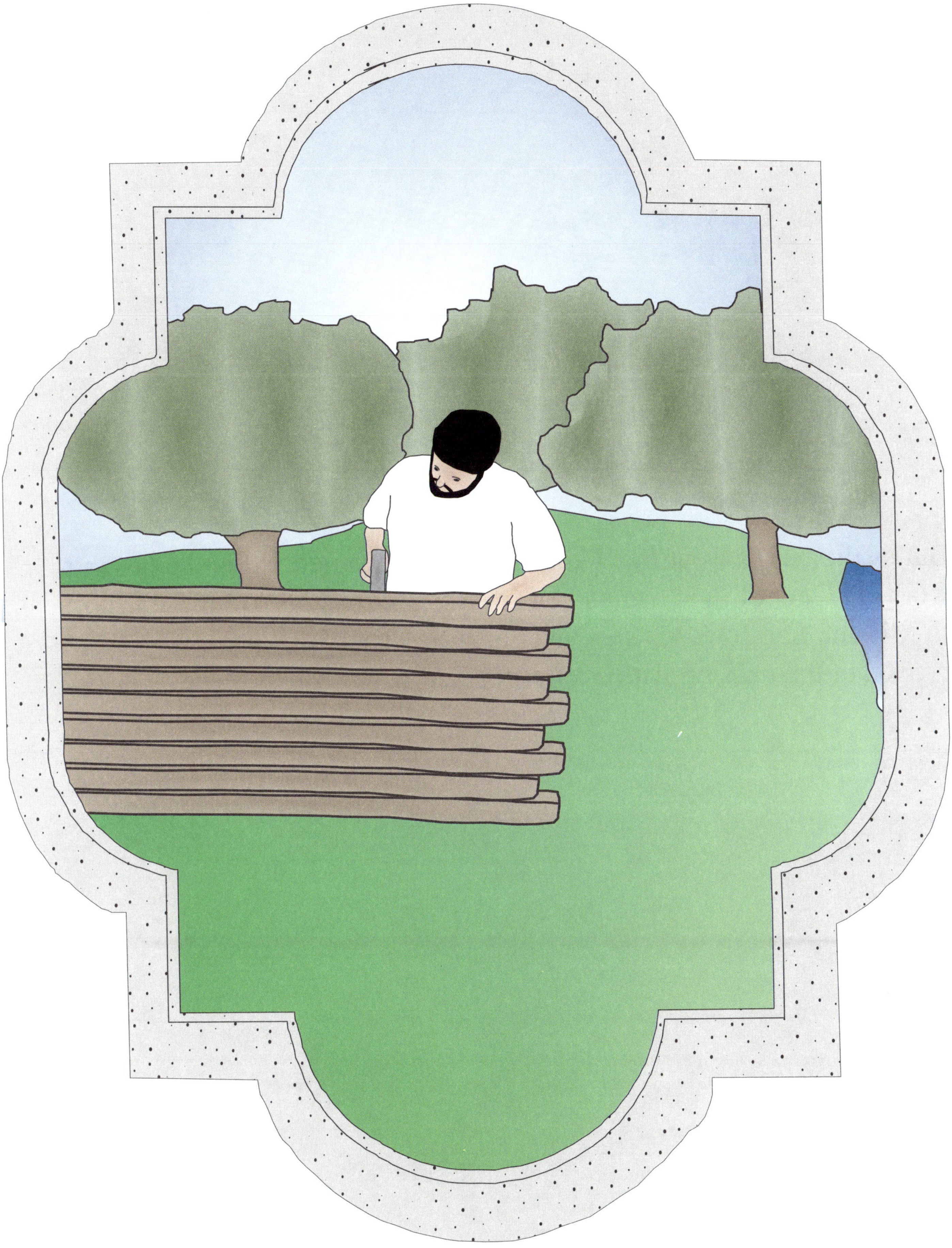

But as the weeks went by , Pedro waited and waited. Soon he began to worry. Plenty of time had passed for Rosa to make the journey from Spain to Mission San José, but she never arrived. Then one day, a messenger arrived at the mission with a letter for Pedro.

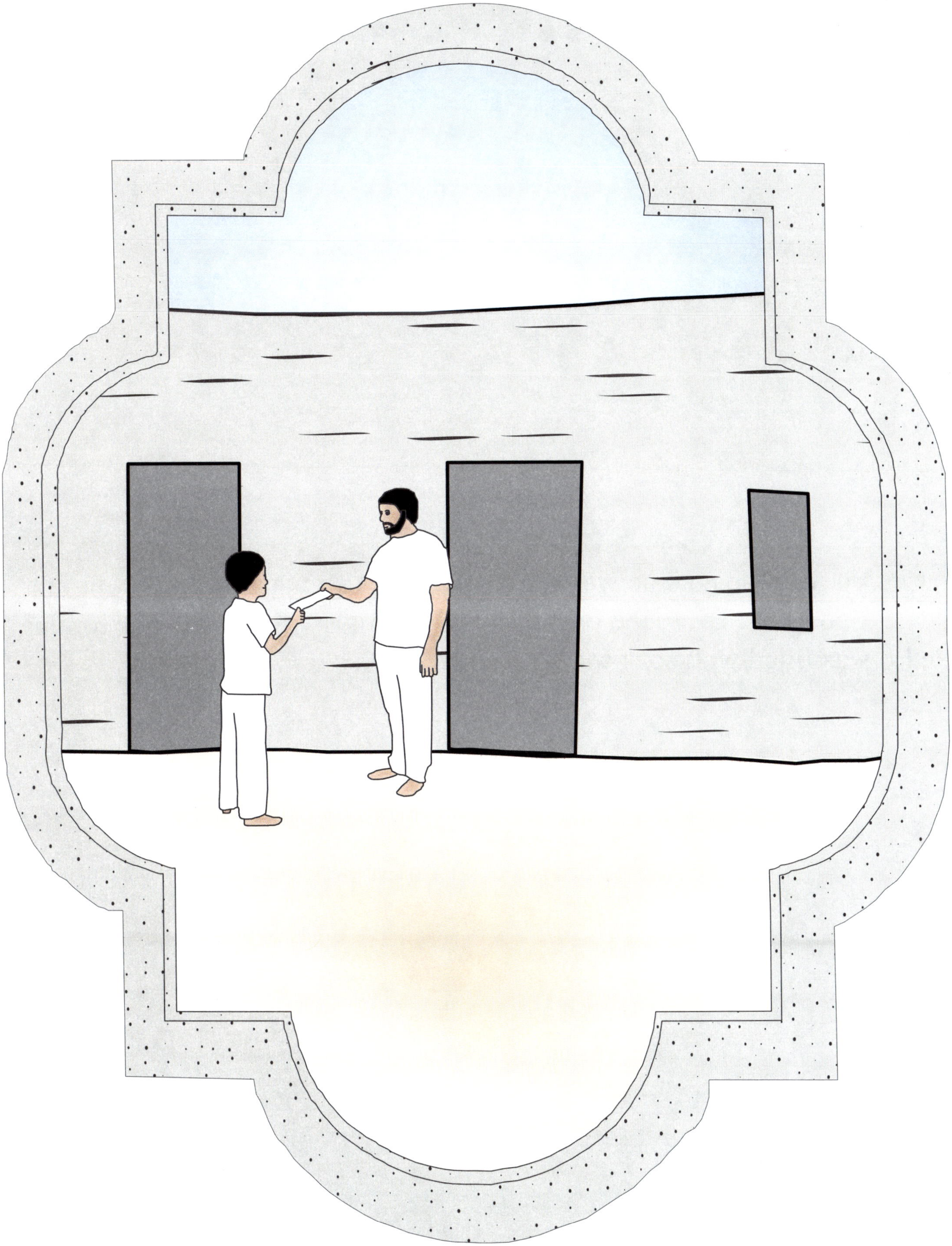

As Pedro read the note he was stunned. Rosa's ship had been caught in a storm, and sank. Everyone on board had been lost. Rosa was not coming. Pedro was filled with sorrow.

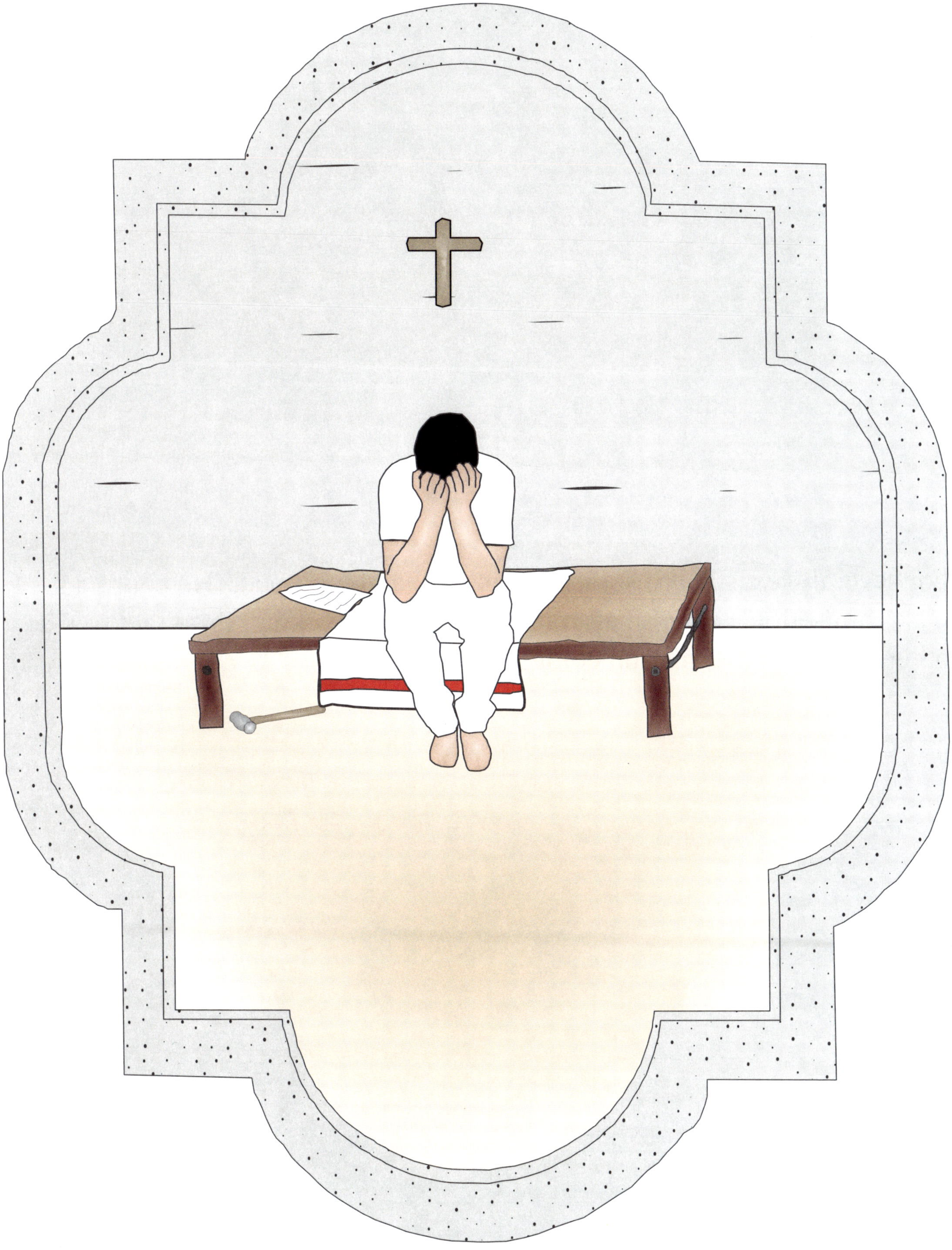

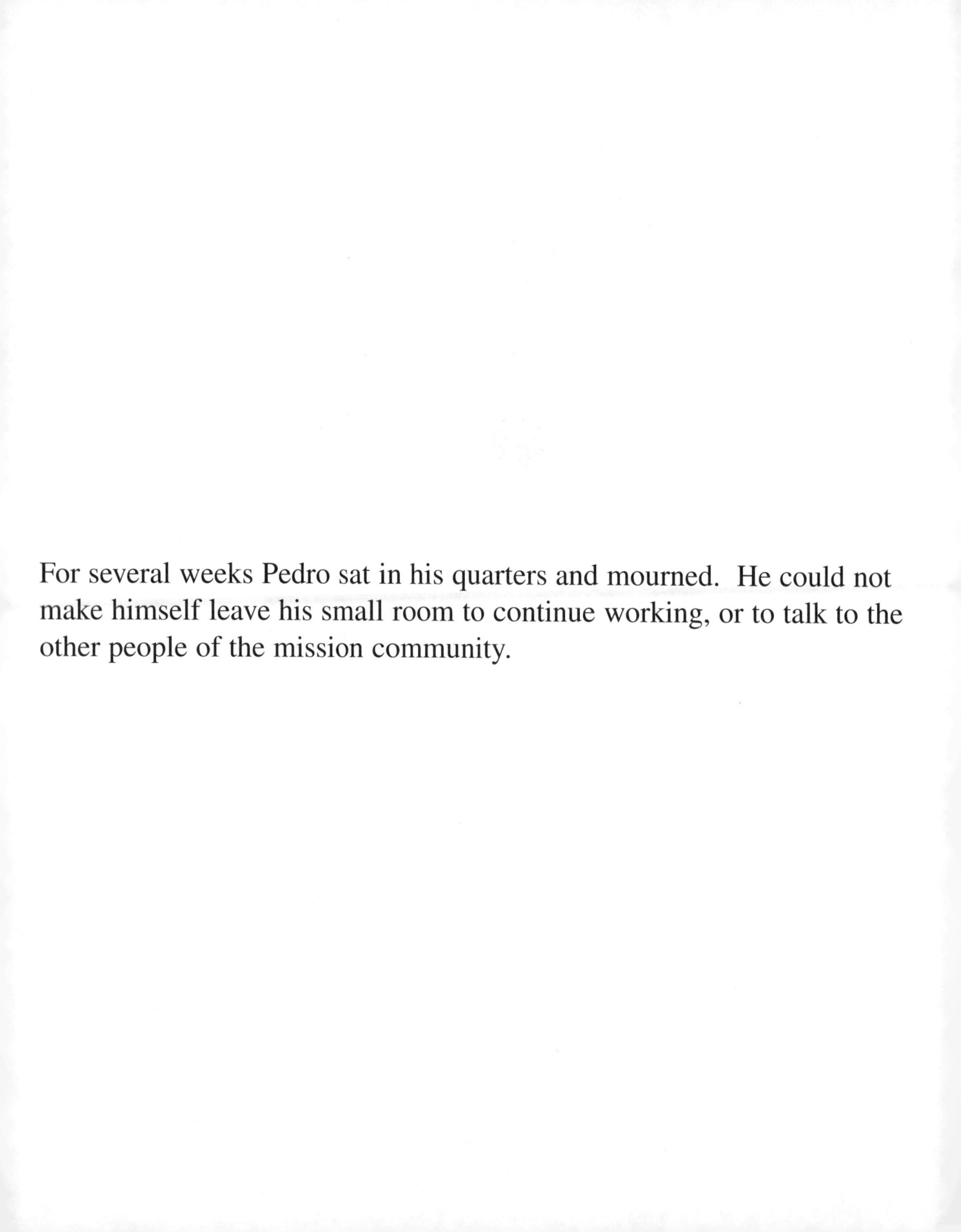

For several weeks Pedro sat in his quarters and mourned. He could not make himself leave his small room to continue working, or to talk to the other people of the mission community.

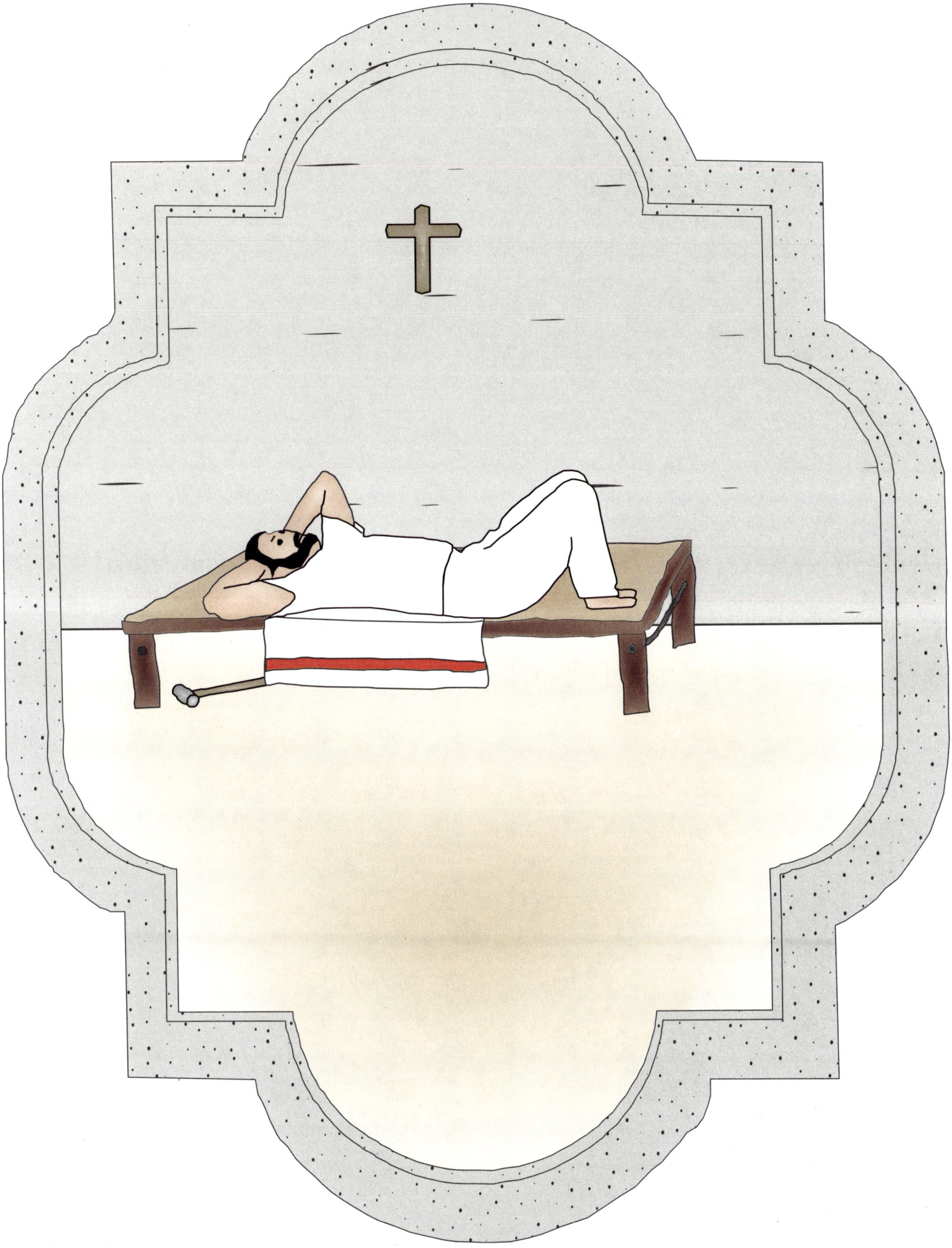

Then one day, one of the priests of the mission came to visit Pedro. "Pedro," the priest said, "I know your sorrow is great. Losing Rosa is the worst thing that has ever happened to you. Yet, you need to find a way to express your love for her in other ways."

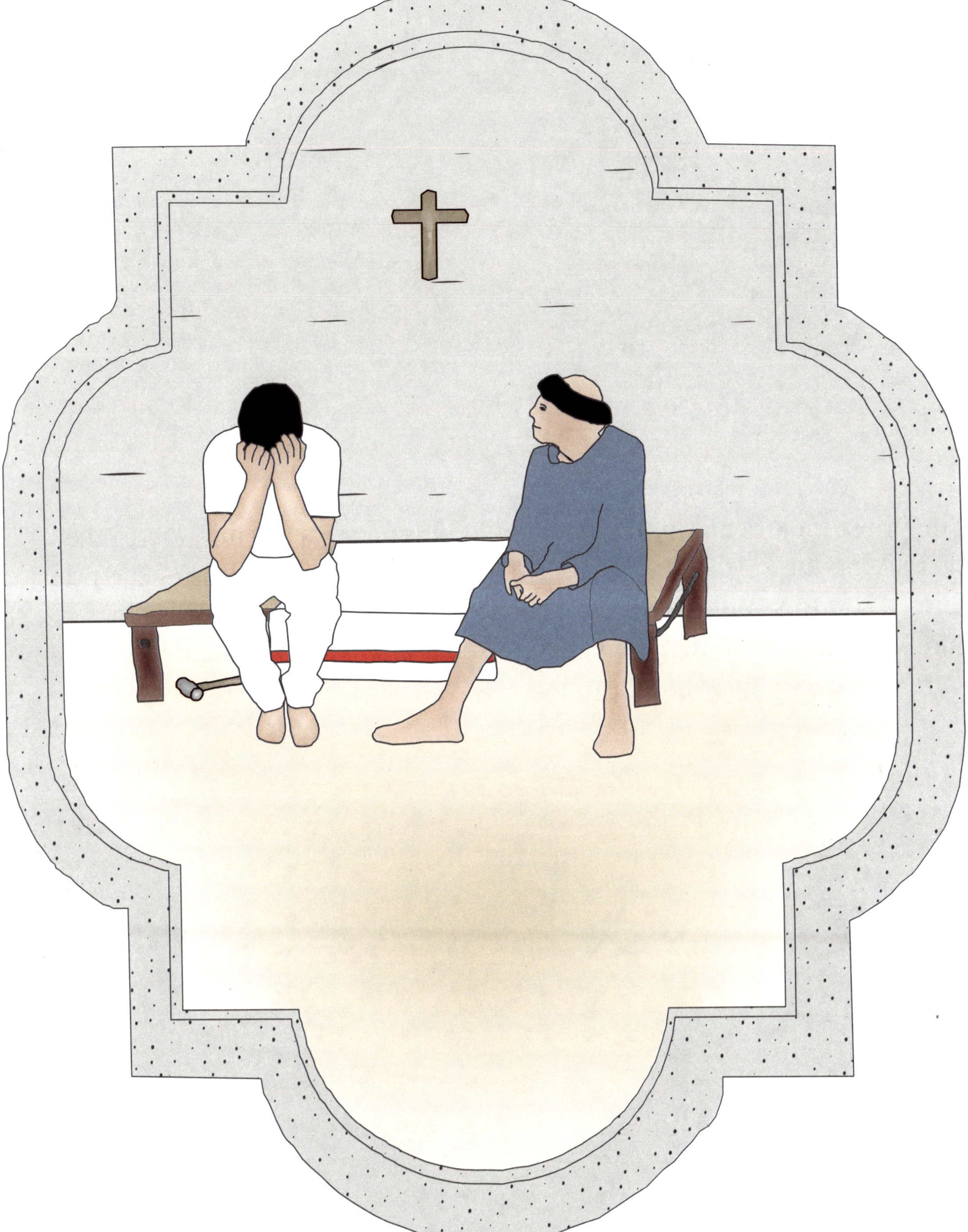

The priest took Pedro by the hand an led him across the mission to the sacristy on the side of the church. "Make something for Rosa," the priest said. "Use this wall to express your love for her." At first Pedro was not sure what to do, but then he began to see a picture in his mind. He slowly started to carve away at the stone.

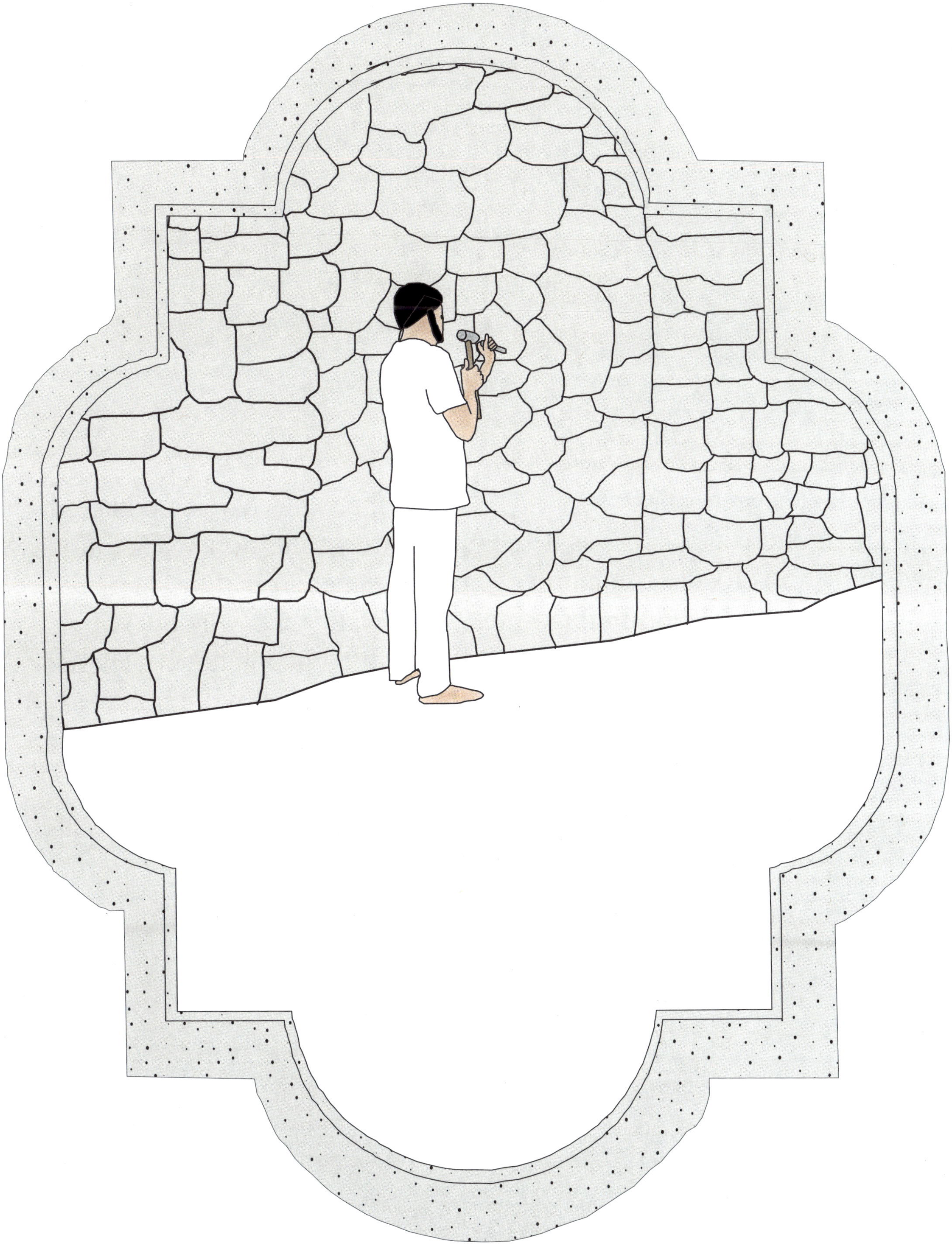

For the next several weeks Pedro worked on the wall. No one bothered him, and he remained silent as he chipped away at the stone. Then finally, it was finished. As the community began to gather around the sacristy wall, they were amazed. In the center of the wall was a window with a beautiful frame carved into the stone surrounding the window. "This is Rosa's Window," Pedro said. "Every time I look at it, I will remember her."

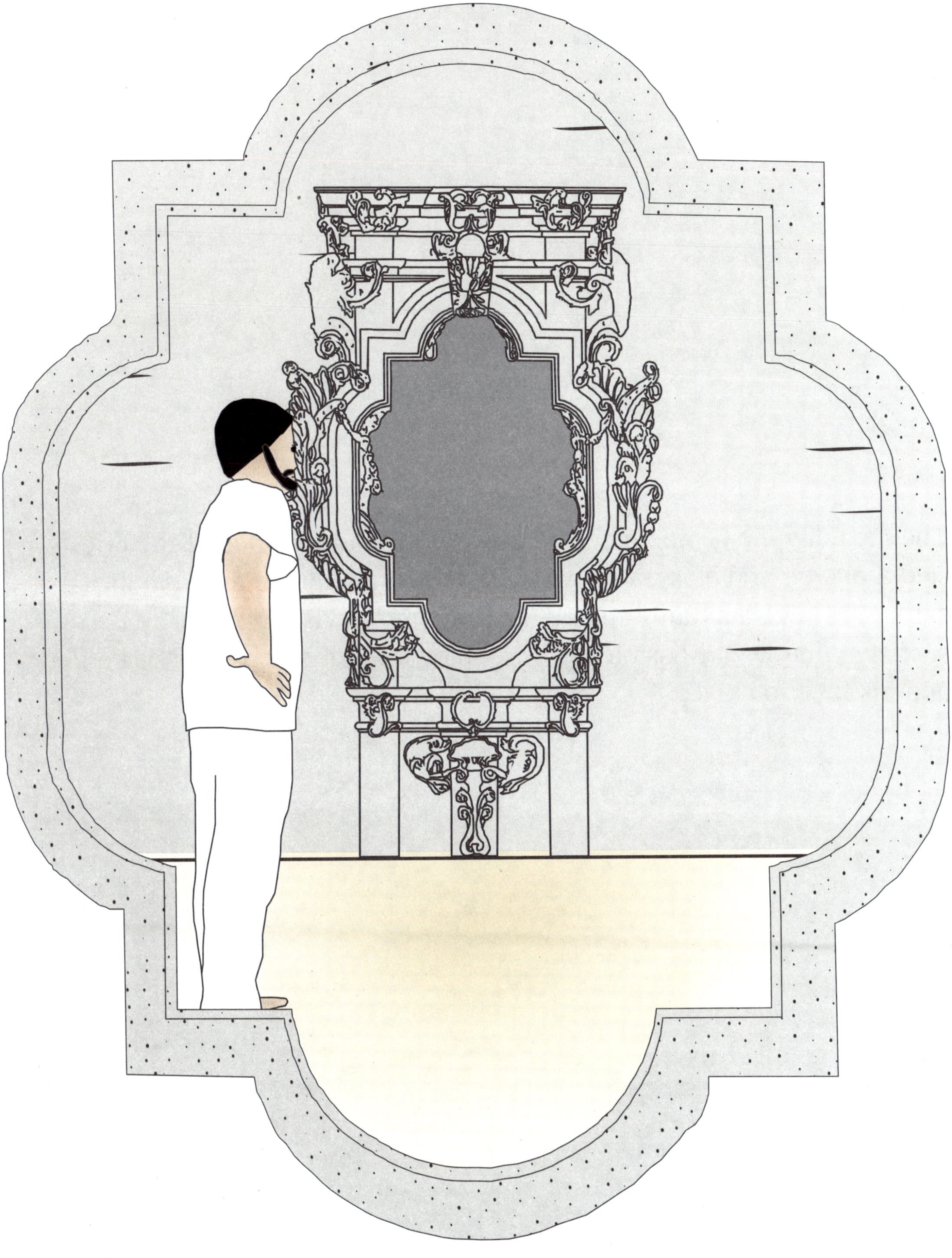

The next day the people gathered at Rosa's Window. One of the priests said a prayer, and blessed the window. They all agreed to remember it as a symbol of love and faithfulness. Even today, as visitors walk by the sacristy window at Mission San José, they are often reminded of Pedro, and his love for Rosa.

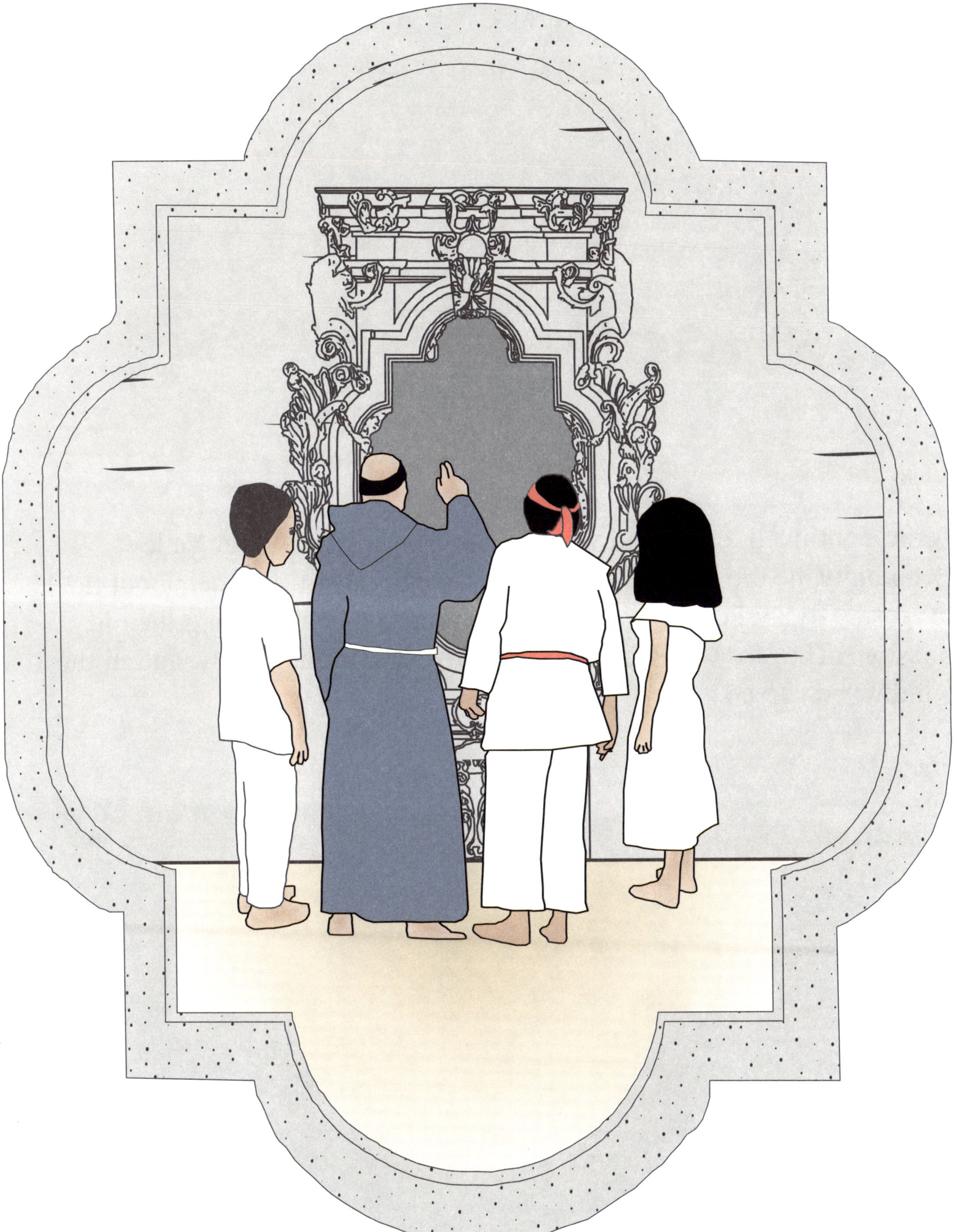

Pedro continued to live and work in the San Antonio River Valley. Eventually, he did start a family, even though he still felt sad about the loss of Rosa. Today Pedro's relatives live in the area surrounding the old mission. The story of Pedro and Rosa lives on in his family, and in the window he carved.

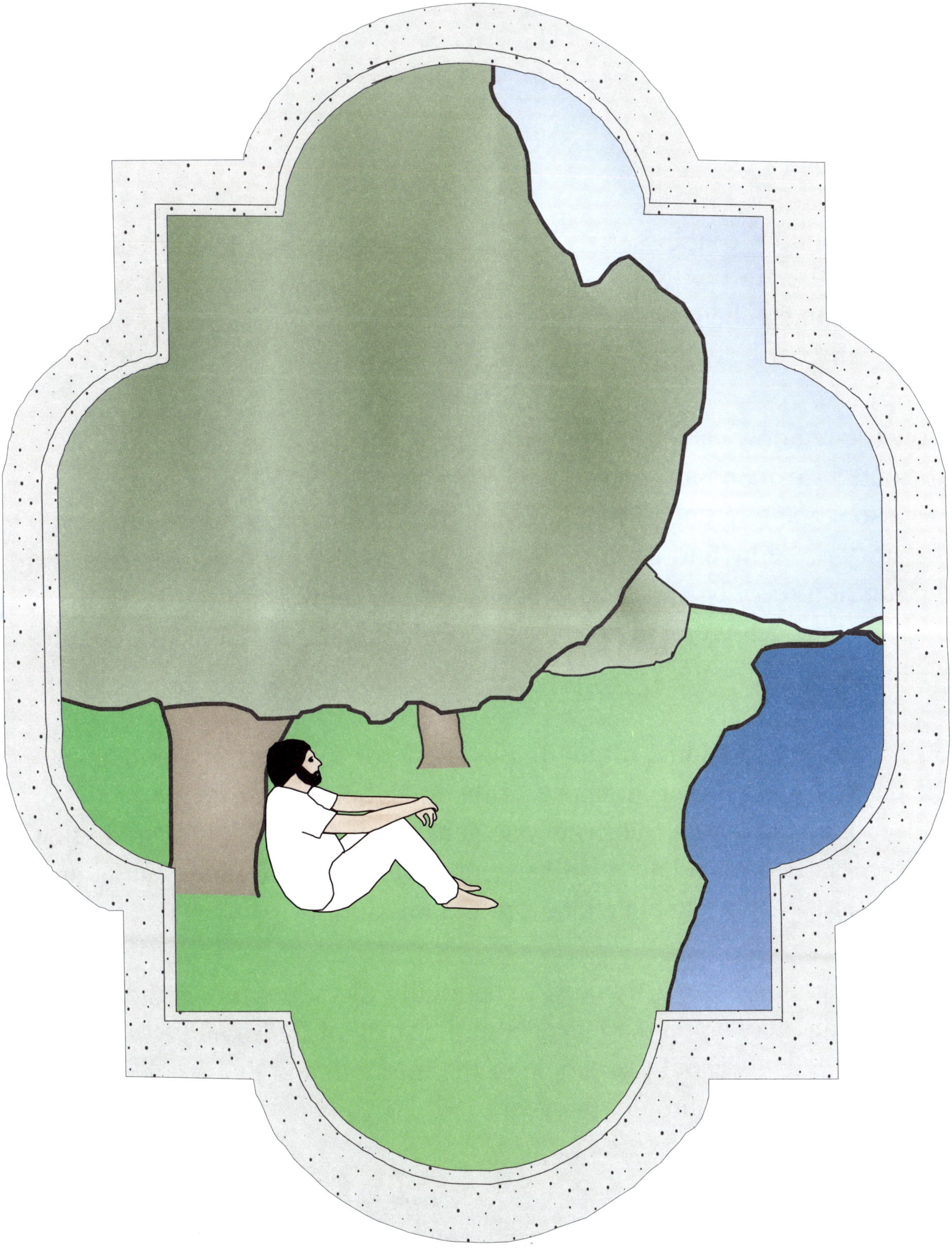

About the Story

Rosa's Window, or the sacristy window, at Mission San José is one of the most popular sites within the San Antonio missions. Many visitors, not knowing much about the missions themselves, arrive wanting to see this beautifully carved window.

How the window came to be is still a matter of question. Some people attribute it to Juan Salizar who was a stone sculptor at the missions. There are also some references in the mission records that tend to disagree with the story of Pedro and Rosa. Pedro is listed as a carpenter and surveyor in the mission records, and it is not known if he had the ability to create such a large stone sculpture. There are also some questions about when Pedro was actually at the mission.

Still, the story of Pedro carving the window for Rosa has endured since the days of the mission. It is one of the most beloved stories in San Antonio, and has been told from one generation to the next for more than 200 years. Pedro's relatives still live in the area around the mission, and are living legacy of this inhabitant of the mission.

Legends do not necessarily need to be totally factual to tell us the truth. While some may argue the facts about the story of Pedro and Rosa, the story still tells us about the people of the mission, and the people who have told this story through the years.